# Copyright

Break & Bloom

© Trisha Leigh Shufelt

Text & images copyright Trisha Leigh Shufelt ©2022

Cover Design Art by Trisha Leigh Shufelt

All rights reserved. No part of this book or images may be re-produced or utilized in any form or by any means, electronic or mechanical, including photocopying, recording or by any information storage and retrieval system, without the prior written permission of the author/artist

# Break & Bloom

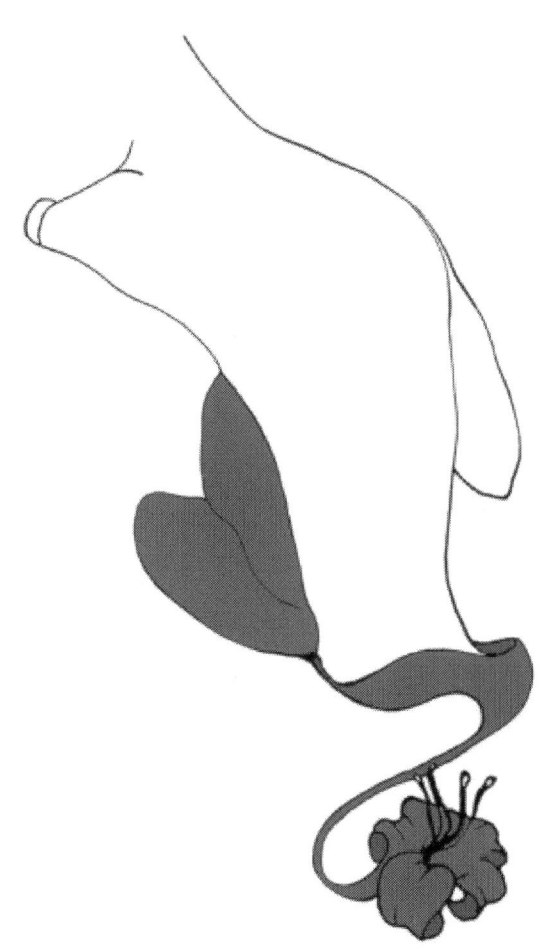

*"Rosebuds are growing through.
Sanguinary visits to the abyss may have
caused this heart to bloom after all."*

*S.A. Quinox*

*Immortalis*

# Dedication

To my husband Andy, who has never given me a reason to break but always gives me reasons to bloom.

# Foreword

The book you're holding in your hand may well be the best purchase you've made all year. When I was asked to write this foreword, I'll admit I found the task somewhat daunting; poetry, more than other genres, can be difficult to quantify. When it's done well, it is an art form unto itself. Poetry can be transcendent and spiritual; it must be felt more than read, and I wasn't convinced I'd be able to do justice to this fabulous collection.

I first became acquainted with Trisha Leigh Shufelt's work about a year ago, and it was love at first stanza. I'll happily boast that I own the very first printed copy of Shufelt's Liminal Lines, and I was thrilled to hear that she'd released another collection. Being familiar with her work, I had high expectations of Break & Bloom, and this book exceeded every expectation I had of it. Shufelt hypnotizes us with vivid imagery and melodic lyricism. She entices us with her mastery of the rules of writing, and then she leaves us awestruck as she artfully breaks every rule with flair. Her style has the precise, deliberate sort of irreverence that is the hallmark of a true artist. These pages are drenched in love, righteous rage, agony, heartache, and hope. She fearlessly and unapologetically breaks our hearts with pieces like Haunted, gives us hope with The Key, makes us self-reflect with No, and in every piece, she invites us to see a part of ourselves a bit differently than we had before. May you experience this collection as profoundly as I have.

Mira Hadlow
Author-As Muses Burn

## About Break & Bloom

Writing poetry can be a cathartic personal journey. It's like ripping the band-aid off an unhealed wound and hoping it won't hurt. When 2020 and Covid isolation rolled around, I, like so many others, experienced intense anxiety. While I was finding newfound artistic success, inside, I was spiraling out of control. I needed to do something, but I couldn't see the forest for the trees. Furthermore, I couldn't find a therapist. So, I did what I've always done. I immersed myself in my writing and art. But a funny thing happened. Instead of writing fantasy stories and painting, I began writing poetry. Doing so opened a channel to the past, and a means to heal.

The poems in Break & Bloom reflect my 2015 cancer journey, relationships with others, myself, spirituality, addiction, depression, and unresolved aspects of my childhood. It's a book about survival in every sense of the word. I hadn't written any poetry since I was a teenager, and back then, it was poetry about the moon and June. At 52, I was more than a little surprised to start writing poetry and even more shocked at the amount of unresolved pain I hadn't acknowledged in my years on this planet. However, I soon discovered that poetry was a way for me to give a voice to my past and find closure in ways I never imagined. It helped ground me while reeling in some of the uncontrollable chaos through the structure of my thoughts and words. Robert Frost said, "I have never started a poem yet whose end I knew. Writing a poem is discovering." No truer words were ever spoken. So, when I decided to create this book, I thought, what do I want to discover and uncover about myself?

Break & Bloom is a visceral book about standing naked before the world, hoping to be seen, heard, and healed. Not everything I write will resonate. Sometimes I write short little ditties. Other poems are longer and more introspective. Some of my poems may trigger unresolved pain within yourself. I beg you to examine those feelings and ask the hard questions. That is what I do every day as an artist. I've never been one to sugar-coat my feelings or write poems to motivate the masses. I'm no one's guru and always have been a work in progress. When we stop learning about ourselves, we are doomed to wither. How's that for motivation? Okay, I can do better. I hope my words help others who may feel silenced but want to shout from the rooftops of their soul.

Trisha Leigh

# In the Garden

## Seeds

| | |
|---|---|
| Dance | 24 |
| Torch | 25 |
| Blurred Lines | 26 |
| Listen | 28 |
| Stone Pillow | 29 |
| Pulpit | 30 |
| Shadow Walks | 32 |
| Search | 33 |
| Cycles | 34 |
| Travel Guide | 35 |
| Distraction | 36 |
| Junk Drawer | 37 |
| Question | 38 |
| Spinderella | 39 |
| Speak | 40 |
| Maeve | 41 |
| Dreams | 42 |

| | |
|---|---|
| Safe | 43 |
| Shadow Dance | 44 |
| To Feel | 45 |
| Beautiful Boy | 46 |
| Uninvited | 47 |
| Charlie & Nicky | 48 |
| You Divine Spark | 50 |
| Garden of Hope | 51 |

## Weeds

| | |
|---|---|
| Naked | 54 |
| Pandora's Box | 55 |
| Pretty in Pink | 56 |
| Thoughts & Prayers | 58 |
| Are you listening? | 59 |
| Little Girl Lost | 60 |
| Why the Partridge no Longer Soars | 62 |
| Unsaid | 64 |

| | |
|---|---|
| Answer Me | 65 |
| Put to Rest | 66 |
| Once Upon a Time... | 68 |
| Reflection | 69 |
| The Key | 70 |
| Would You? | 72 |
| Girl Interrupted | 74 |
| Addiction | 76 |
| The Stuff in the Middle | 77 |
| Oh, the places you will go | 78 |
| Thief | 79 |
| Seasons | 80 |
| Fisher Kings | 84 |
| A Rant | 86 |
| Girl with the Wayward Soul | 90 |
| River Song | 92 |
| Mantra | 94 |
| Over | 95 |
| Alone | 96 |

Shufelt-Break & Bloom

| | |
|---|---|
| Scream | 97 |
| Vacation | 98 |
| Choices | 100 |
| Trust | 101 |

## Thorns

| | |
|---|---|
| Diagnosis | 104 |
| Reign | 105 |
| The Fool's Journey | 106 |
| Breadcrumbs | 112 |
| Speak to Me | 114 |
| Sabotage | 115 |
| Balance | 116 |
| Perfect | 117 |
| Turn | 118 |
| Escape | 119 |
| No More | 120 |
| Punch-drunk | 123 |

| | |
|---|---|
| Cracked | 124 |
| Once Upon a Time | 126 |
| Cold Girl | 127 |
| Screaming Silent | 128 |
| Pedestal | 129 |
| Anxiety's Pull | 130 |
| War | 131 |
| Grief | 132 |
| Safe Place | 133 |
| Empty | 134 |
| Missing | 135 |
| From P to M | 136 |
| Rabbit Soup | 138 |
| Hers | 140 |
| Predictive Text Poetry | 141 |
| Haunted | 142 |
| Soul Searching | 144 |
| Survivor | 146 |

Moonstruck     147

Precious Things     148

Avoidance     149

# Blooms

Andrew     152

Stories     153

Gemels     154

The Allegory of Secret Places     155

Elements     156

The Promises of Evermore     158

You     160

Stargaze     161

Wanderlust     162

Patrick     163

Eternal     164

October Gives Birth     165

Rain     166

| | |
|---|---|
| Healing | 167 |
| Poisoned | 168 |
| Razor | 170 |
| Surrender | 171 |
| Girl in a Box | 172 |
| Umbra | 174 |
| Goals | 175 |
| Swallow | 176 |
| Here | 178 |
| No | 179 |
| Forgiveness | 180 |
| Weave World | 181 |
| With or Without You | 182 |
| Solitude | 183 |
| I Wish for Silence | 184 |
| Rise | 186 |
| Looking in the Mirror | 187 |
| Art of Pain | 188 |

Shufelt-Break & Bloom

| | |
|---|---|
| Art of Healing | 189 |
| Break & Bloom | 190 |
| First Frost | 192 |
| Death is a Collector | 194 |
| Kintsukuroi | 195 |
| Doubt | 196 |
| Battle Ground | 197 |
| January | 198 |
| Baggage | 199 |
| Aching Wisdom | 200 |
| Queen of Hell | 201 |
| Warrior | 202 |
| To be a Book | 204 |
| Wonderland Never Dies | 206 |

# Seeds

Dance

I stand en pointe upon the precipice
of possibility, balanced
betwixt retreat
and the leap.

I stare down,
fearful at the
face of what if.

She gazes up at
me, afraid
I will call her
bluff

        and
    take a
    dance.

## Torch

What draws one to chaos?
Is it what draws the moth to the flame?
The need to burn,
to feel,
to touch the forbidden,
and awaken it within ourselves.

## Blurred Lines

Fear is a lesson
first learned from rejection.

That violent push
from the loving womb
into the virgin unknown.

We cry out, invaded
by the ringing knell
of our voice.

We reach,
hands flailing and clawing
into frigid nothingness.

We search with eyes
shocked from shadow
into the bright
plethora of possibilities.

To silence the noise.
To grasp for what was lost.
To see why we are here.

Shufelt-Break & Bloom

Always searching
for a way back
to trust.

# Listen

What befalls the self,
awakens the Soul's wisdom
if one is willing to hear the words.

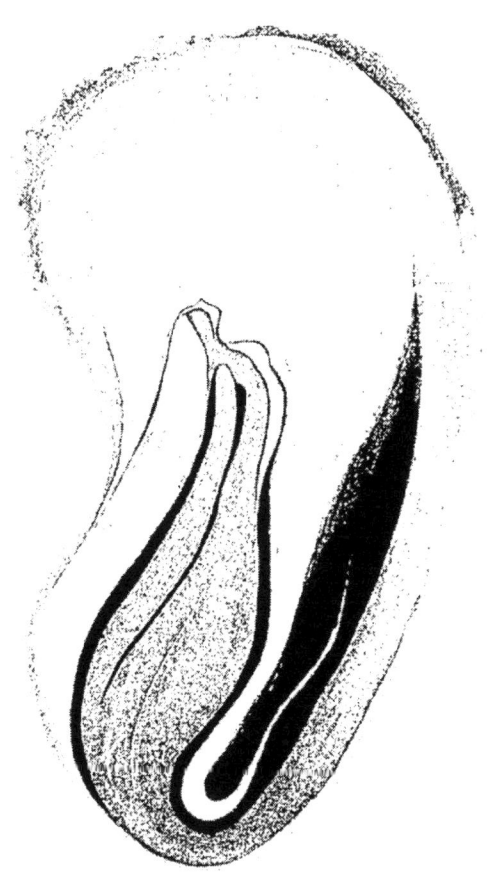

## Stone Pillow (1992)

Father would drive past them every day,
Lifeless bodies that slept on steam grates.
"God has cheated you," he said.

He showed me the ones whose homes were cardboard coffins.
Others made their living by begging for a few quarters to make it through the day.

In a land so rich, why can't these people afford a cup of coffee?

Newspapers telling of daily events crush namelessly beneath their swollen feet.

Faceless, she kept all her possessions in a shopping card-all her life stories rolling over a stone pillow.

Nameless, his only friend was a bottle.

Life has made you its lowest common denominator.

What apologies could we give?

# Pulpit

Under the skin is a highway of sin.
That is what I heard him say.
I looked around and began to drown
in thoughts that might carry me away.

He slammed his fist and did insist
we would all burn in hell.
It awakened his sheep from their glazy sleep
back to the throes of his spell.

"Sinners," he shouted, blustered, and touted,
shaking his little black book in the air.
His parishioners nodded, pouted, but lauded,
lifting their hands in heavenly prayer.

I shifted and sighed
as his eyes fixed upon mine.
It wasn't guilt of sin but anger within.
What gave him the power of the Divine?

Was it that little black book
that got him off the hook
while the rest of us were damned?
I couldn't resist and shook my fist,
standing before the man.

Shufelt-Break & Bloom

The flock turned on me in righteous glee
as the preacher blustered and pointed
and cast me out without question or doubt,
I was no longer God's anointed.

"Fine with me. God's grace is free!"
I shouted, raising my fist toward the sky.
No church or preacher would be my teacher.
I didn't need his pulpit of lies.

Whatever befell, be it Heaven or Hell,
whatever the path would be,
I never looked back in fear or lack,
for the Divine was always within me.

## Shadow Walks

Shadow walks behind us in resistance.
It walks in front of us for control.
It hides inside of us at a distance
yet craves the light of the Soul.

It longs
to walk
beside us,
balanced
in
between
the
darkness
and the
light of
us,
wishing to
be seen.

## Search

I am traveling
as I have in other lifetimes,
always searching for the home I'd lost-

always longing for a way back to me.

# Cycles

Through the never is leading me back to whatever, never, I never resolved.

# Travel Guide

I had a Social Science professor in college whose name escapes me. Yet, sewn into the tapestry of my brain is a vivid memory, like a thread from one of her tattered rugs. Within it weaves a sensory overload of walnut-stained wood tables covered in vibrant silken scarves and a fortune teller's dream of lipstick-stained teacups embellished with dried tealeaf remnants. Ancient vanilla-scented poetry books competing with her curried lunch hang heavy in the air. Everyone thought she was eccentric; some even called her crazy. To me, she was the epitome of culture and wisdom, a dog-eared travel guide I was fortunate to stumble upon while backpacking through life.

# Distraction

Tell me lies covered in chocolate decadence
while I sink into the velvety distraction
of purple prose dripping with verbosity.

## Junk Drawer

My grandmother had a catch-all drawer in an old China cabinet.

Inside were odd items, candy bars, crayons, skeleton keys, whatchamacallits, and thingamajigs.

It was a magical place first explored by my step-sister and me upon entering her house.

She called it a doohickey drawer.

I have a junk drawer.

It is far less magical.

# Question

Why do we worship at the feet of fear yet turn a blind eye to the salvation in trust?

## Spinderella

Spider spins a silken web,
weaving art from her lacy bobbin.

What mysteries does she watch and keep
in her threads, so silver sodden?

What nightmares do those despair
when wrapped in her woven cocoon?

Or do they sleep a peaceful rest
beneath the gleaming midnight moon?

# Speak

Years ago, I taught children speech.
It was a job I fell into.
It was a job I loved more than words could convey.
It came in and out of my life-
a transient passage of time
like a soul mate with a life lesson.

For many years I struggled to understand why it fell into my lap and why it had to leave.
Then one day, when I couldn't find the words, I realized it came along to teach me to give a voice to other children when the child in me couldn't speak.

## Maeve

Like a seductive spider weaving a silky web, she embodied a wicked beauty, seeming to possess all the darkness of an evil nightmare one was willing to experience just to share her space.

# Dreams

Dreams allow us to explore our subconscious mind to answer questions we fear to ask when awake.

## Safe

There is a hiraeth in solitude only the survivor understands.
There is safety and healing in its silence.

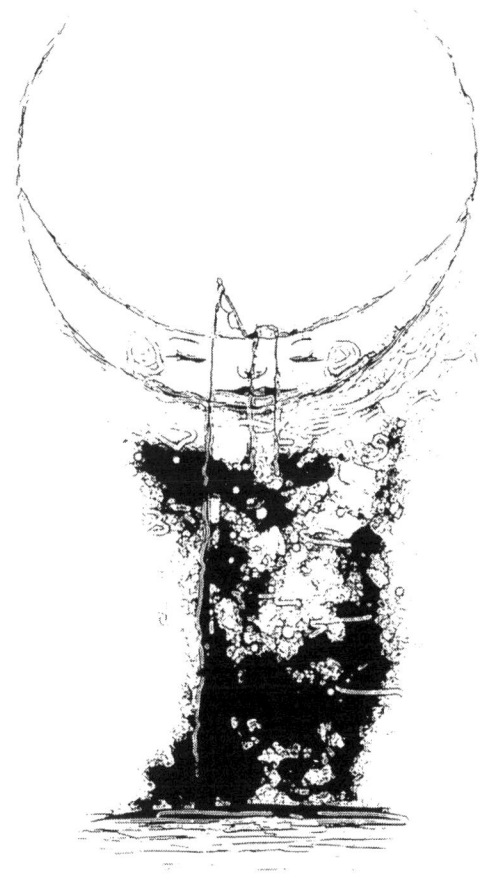

## Shadow Dance

May the darkness dance with my shadows while my soul awakens to the dawn.

## To Feel

I feel numb,
as numb as my fingers
and toes on a winter's day.
Floating on the wind
like a balloon with no direction,
unprepared for the fall.
And yet I fall,
as inevitable as rain on a hot summer day,

      I

                fall.

And in that fall,
I feel,
feel so deeply my bones vibrate.

I wonder if this awakening is truth?

And so, I seek the things
that shake my bones and stir my blood,
knowing the risk
but caring little of the danger.

Only in those moments,

I feel alive.

# Beautiful Boy

My darling boy,
the darkness inside of you
is no match for the light
you blaze upon the world.

## Uninvited

If I give it a name,
it won't be a stranger.

If I try to understand it,
it won't be something to fear.

If I own it,
I can destroy it.

Charlie & Nicky

We were best friends, old souls connected by the threads of time, pop music, bad choices, beautiful boys, and innocence lost.

I remember sitting on the hood of your mother's car, talking about the future between puffs of stolen cigarettes and sips of schnapps.

I remember taking the long way home from school, so we could spend our lunch money on bridal magazines and bad 80s fashion.

We talked about being rich, being loved...being seen.

We hung out at the local bowling alley, crushing on guys who were much too old for us.

We were thrilled by the chase but frightened of the burn.

Shufelt-Break & Bloom

We were so unaware of the thin, dangerous line we walked.

I imagine the bowling alley is gone now, replaced by a Walmart or some other business.

Gone is the naivete of youth and those beautiful, dangerous boys we thought would complete our world.

I imagine they are old men now who don't even remember our names.

Still, we remain connected through time, buried memories, and all that is newly found.

## You Divine Spark

If I could impart any words of wisdom upon you, it would be to grant yourself the grace you give without hesitation to others.

Allow yourself to live beyond the limits of perfect timing.

And remember to see the sacred in everything, including yourself.

## Garden of Hope

I planted seeds of trust that what returned would be blooms of hope.

# Weeds

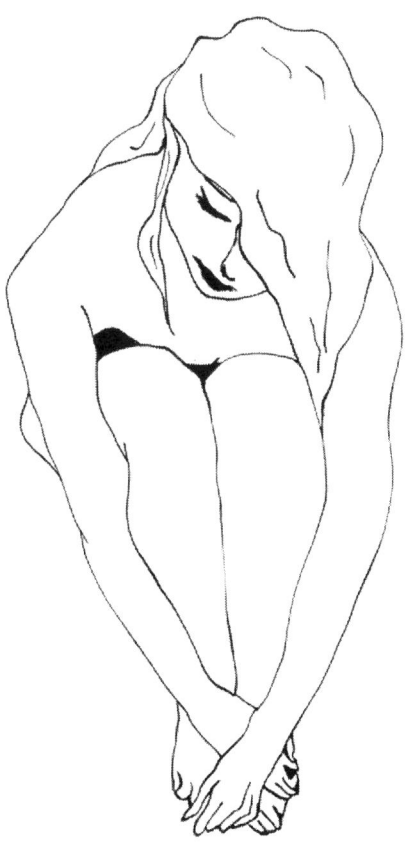

## Naked

They love your outside,
judging your book by its cover.
But will they still feel the same
when you split
your seams wide open,
exposing your demons
with dogeared pages
and smudged, inky edits
for all the world to see?

## Pandora's Box

I have opened it
all the beautiful, dark things,
hidden, not in a box but in a reticent portal
a rabbit's hole of pent-up poisons
a sarcophagus of candlelit rooms
and inky black thoughts
a place where I fail to breathe
but desire to live
a place where I fear I may lose my sanity
in the quest for my awakening

## Pretty in Pink

You were my Duckie, and I was your Andie.
We were pretty in pink until we weren't.

You made me laugh.
You were always making people laugh.
Except when you were quiet, retreating into dark places, I could not follow.

I didn't want to follow you.

You thought it was because I didn't care.
I cared more than your denial would admit.
I knew the danger of your dark places.
If I didn't explore them with you, I was safe.

The truth was, I was never safe-
not even when you made me laugh.

Trust becomes a noose in the hands of the wrong person.

That night, I trusted you.

That night, you convinced me,
I was the one who hung myself
with your rope.

## Thoughts and Prayers

Save a prayer if it's filled with lies.
Save a prayer if it's deceit in disguise.

I have no use for your latent words
and hypocritical posturing.
Prayer is not an excuse for Divine
intervention while doing nothing.

If God gave us free will
and the Divine is within,
let he who casts the first stone
be free of all sin.

For if God exists,
it is not to intervene
but to let us understand our connection,
our oneness, unseen.

So, if you want an answered prayer
or need a sign or a key,
get out of your fucking chair
and be the change you wish to see.

Rise to the occasion
of who you are meant to be.
That is prayer in action.
An answer of divinity.

## Are you listening?

covered in gold
mouth open in a defiant awe shape
tongue the color of cranberries
I hear your voice keening
in my head

you are dying
in an arsenal of words
rolling over your skin
dropping from the sky
unloading from a barrel

you are screaming
for peace
a moments peace

I wonder if they ever heard you,
or will you only echo in reverb?

it wasn't me
it's not real
but they're still fighting
and you're still crying

in my head
in your head
you are screaming
they're still dying

# Little Girl Lost

I remember her-
little girl with large doe eyes and long mousey hair, riding a green bicycle with a daisy-flowered banana boat seat in the pouring summer rain.

She was fond of baking mudpies and other earthly delights on hot concrete for imaginary guests while saving bottles of pop and peanut butter sandwiches on Wonder Bread for herself.

I remember she liked to explore backwoods mountains in search of empty whisky bottles and hillbilly treasures.

She had blackened and callused foot soles; no bee sting could penetrate.

She liked to collect sweetgum pods, make daisy chains, and blow grass blades between her thumbs.

Somewhere between truth and fiction, she is hiding.

Somewhere between boys and heartbreak, she is giving pieces of herself away.

Somewhere between being told what she can and cannot be has stripped herself bare of trying.

Somewhere between what was and what will never be, she is disappearing.

I suppose it's inevitable, trading muddy hands for muddled thoughts-
trading daisy chains for another type of chain, invisible and without a key.

Eventually, living on in the laughter of other children.

## Why the Partridge No Longer Soars

I used to love the smell of woodsmoke, but not anymore, not after what the Partridge did.

Rabbits no longer dance in the burned-out chaparral now filled with the dead's ash.

When I confronted you, you groused at me under gray skies, and your voice became like a singing saw to your crocodile tears, leaving the deed to scent my memories and the rain to molder the rest.

I could see the lies behind your eyes-
a message.

> Sometimes poisons make a home
> in the fairest things.

When I prayed for justice, the smoke-scented breeze blew from the blue heavens leaving blackened poetry at my feet,

"All is well. All is well."

I realized the dead also knew what the Partridge did, and Karma would take care of the rest.

*References the Last Taschastas by Joaquin Miller 1888

## Unsaid

Too many unspoken words died behind her caged teeth.

The weight swelled on her tongue until she was forced to swallow them in self-preservation.

Those days the unsaid words became invisible scars, weaving their way under her skin to make a home in her heart.

Shufelt-Break & Bloom

## Answer me

I am a disobedient child playing with matches, igniting neurons to flame, and the only way to breathe is your response, extinguishing the anxious fires within my mind.

## Put to Rest

You don't remember me,
but I remember *you*.

First grade, Myrtle.
Third grade, Jeanoux.
Fifth grade, Georgia.
Seventh grade, Sarah.
And the three nameless girls who followed me home from school that crisp autumn day.

I remember the hair pulling, the bloody elbows, and that sick incident in the girl's bathroom I should have reported but didn't.

I remember your diatribes-
simple words that slid off your callow tongues with ease but lacked the substance of life experience.

Eventually, I buried you-all of you.
But first, I had to dig deep for the secret of why you picked me.

It was hidden in plain sight-
an insecurity without a lock-

an inconspicuous weed-
in your garden of torment-
a nutrient you lacked
but found copious within me.

Despite your well-tended efforts to break
me, I flourished with indifference and
choked off your insidious rot at the root-

Destroying in you what you failed to harvest
from me.

# Once Upon a Time...

I believe in fairytales.

Not the happily ever after kind, but those inked from darkness, with knife-edged warnings about evil lurking behind fair faces.

I believe in them because they exist.

Our ancestors knew the power behind the stories, which is why they shared them.

Over time, their words became watered-down, fanciful tales about handsome princes and grand castles.

Wolves who exchanged sugar-coated lies for a peek at our goody baskets.

Instead of saying no, they taught us to share because no one likes a rude little girl.

## Reflection

When did these bones begin to ache?
When did these lines first appear?
What does it matter?
They were born from living, not dying.

# The Key

What will it take to make you see?
The world does not revolve around you and me.

That what is on the screen is just a facade,
and what is real is closer to God.

We live in a world of fear,
driven by anger, greed, and tears.

Driven by wars, fame, and hate.
Tell me the path to unity isn't too late?

Conspiracy theories poison our minds
while toxins are killing us all in due time.

While corrupt politicians lie
and violence takes hold,
pushing us further
into their fear-driven fold.

I still believe love is the key
to unlock the door
between what is and what can be.

When we stop and see the soul within,
only then can peace begin.

## Would you?

If you could go back in time and have a conversation with your younger self, would you?

What age would you pick?

What moment would you heal, transform, or erase?

I wonder?

I've stood before her in my mind.

Knelt in front of her and stared into her brown eyes-

a little girl, barely six years old, in the pouring rain, watching him drive away.

I've sat next to her on the floor as she stared at the television, hoping the imaginary world within would offer an escape from the harsh reality around her.

I've seen the sorrow in her eyes and felt heartbreak so visceral my rehearsed reclamations full of good intentions only betray me in their cadence.

I have no wisdom to impart.

I have no comfort to give her and choose instead to remain silent.

In truth, I realize she is the one who has healed me.

There are no words or erasures of the past that should alter the lessons only time and experience can impart.

A wound releases no poison unless it is cut.

# Girl Interrupted

you mean nothing
your thoughts are nothing
you're here for pleasure
you're here for pain
you're a toy
your body belongs to me
your thoughts
belong to me
you're dirty
you're a bitch
you're a whore
you're too fat
you're too thin
you're weak
play the game
shut your mouth
wear this
don't wear that
you deserved it
you asked for it
you're too old
you're too young
you're crazy

good girls listen
good girls behave

LIES!

they want to burn you
to own you
to silence you
to tame you
but you...
you are the witches they could not burn
you are creation,
and creation cannot be owned
you are the goddess incarnate,
and goddesses cannot be silenced
you are the Divine spark
connected to the tides and the moon

you are what they cannot tame

the girls they interrupted
who became women
who became the storm they all fear

## Addiction

Bridges over water make me hold my breath.

Deepwater is an abyss I cannot surface.

I always dream I'm drowning
and yet, I pour another drink.

## The Stuff in the Middle

Sometimes I feel like an Oreo cookie with a crumbling outer shell, relying on the crap inside to hold me together while melting under pressure in a glass of cold milk.

## Oh, the places you will go

In the darkness of your head
or lying awake in your bed,
your racing heart skips a beat.
It can even happen on the street.

Scary thoughts can break your day
and make you want to run away.
It's hard to think when filled with fear,
unsure of when IT will appear.

Your feelings are not overblown
despite the times you feel alone.
Trust what you feel others do, too,
while trying to see a pathway through.

Give your anxieties a face and name
but never turn on yourself in blame.
Whether outside or residing inside
when what is real and not-collide.

Thief

They say the first cut is the deepest. I never understood the meaning until I met you and watched you walk away with my heart.

# Seasons

January chases me with a sardonic smile.
She hates me the way she hates summer,
turning her nose up all the while.

What resides in her arsenal?
Her smile twists into a nasty sneer.
An icy snowball bites my skin
as February mocks and leers.

I wipe away the ruby crystals
from my bloody, battered face.
February's eyes dance in delight
as January hastens her chase.

But February's interest quickly wains
in her vain and fickle way.
Little will draw her from her quest
of breaking hearts today.

Now March is a different story,
lamenting, blustery, and blue,
she pushes them both aside,
leaving April to her dew.

Shufelt-Break & Bloom

Gentle April hands her a tissue,
for she, too, is a crier, it seems,
pulling them from her floral skirts
as March continues to scream.

She looks toward April,
who melts January's frozen stare,
and showers her with snowdrops,
crocuses, and care.

January's power is melting
with each passing day
for soon, the sun will shine with joy
when joined by sister May.

She saunters toward us,
seductive in her guise,
and whispers poetic musings
to her blushing June brides.

Then firecracker July
with August blazing bright
show off spectacular colors
to everyone's delight

The noise they make
the ruckus they start
fill the now darkened sky
with smoke and art.

Schoolmarm September
blows on a cool breeze.
Clearing the sky
with her skill and ease.

She reminds the trees
to dance once more
Releasing their colors
to the lush earth's floor.

For October arrives with its thrills and frights,
candied apples and pumpkins alight.

Dark winged ravens
call to the wind
harkening reminders,
the veil has thinned.

November's brief stay
turns the sky somber and still.

Shufelt-Break & Bloom

For the ghosts of December,
call on the winter's chill.

A ringing bell for peace on earth,
forgiveness and kindness,
love, and mirth.

Then the cycle begins once again
as January greets me
with a frigid and vengeful grin.

## Fisher Kings

don't tell us to smile
as though we are here for your
entertainment

don't tell us not to cut our hair
as though it were a tether for your touch

don't tell us how to feel
as though you could know what it's like to
birth the world and watch its demise in your
wake

don't send us unsolicited messages
with insipid blandishments
about our eyes,
our lips,
our bodies
as though we were doll parts
in your collection box

we see you
but not how you see us

we know who you are

you
keyboard stalkers
lurking on poetry boards,
hawking us like prey,
you can't wait to devour

you
fisher kings
casting lines
in search of
broken souls

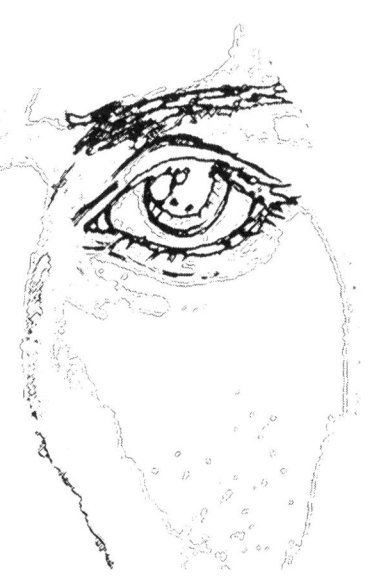

you
collectors
seeking butterflies
to mount
on your fucking
walls

you
wolves in the guise of sheep

as though our peace were your prize

as though we should be grateful for the hunt

# A Rant

The light at the end of the tunnel
is a dream,
a big fucking joke
with no punchline, it seems.
It's the cool kid's lunch table
with no available seat.
The delusion of inclusion,
ripe but not sweet.

Like a moth to a flame,
it attracts but detracts.
A tease and a taste,
it promises but subtracts.

Perpetually,
ironically,
sarcastically,
it deludes
just within reach
depending upon the mood.

It pushes forward
while it leads backward
time and again

to a road once traveled,
not now, but when?
Then?

Hopeful,
mindful,
nose to the grindstone, boastful.
Bust your ass
until bruised and broken,
but never utter never.
No.
That word isn't spoken,
ever.

The failure to achieve
is not the prize to receive.
Keep moving forward
despite its fickle-fated glow.
In a pay-to-play market,
it's not who you know,
not the talent under your belt,
but how much doe you've delt.

Social media is a kid's game,
or so they say.
Either way, I'm too old to care

and too poor to play.

So tired of tripping up,
falling down,
getting back up,
only to sink into the ground
of my mindfuck, pity party
of discontent.
Oh please, just once, let me lament.

Feel abundant,
feel blessed,
just receive.
Saccharine words
I'm too angry to swallow,
hear, or believe.

Besides, I've been there
and done that!
I'm allowed to rant.
That I can control
and eventually recant.

Just for a moment,
let me release it all.
Aren't I entitled to some frustration

Shufelt-Break & Bloom

after I fall?

I'll pick myself up
like I always do
put on a brave face
and muddle through.

I'll dust myself off
and start over once again,
hand in hand with my ego
toward the road that leads to no end.

# Girl with a Wayward Soul

she's a feral cat,
a wayward Soul on a nomad's journey to
leave everything behind

she thinks the grass is greener
in another town,
another city,
maybe even another country,
definitely in someone else's arms

there are no anchors in her pockets holding
her back

the only thing holding her down is regret

she thinks it will not find her, but it finds her

it always finds her like a brand on her skin
she cannot see

and she is a target for her own weaponry

a bullseye

Shufelt-Break & Bloom

she keeps running with horse blinders,
hiding in her art and her make-believe
madness

shrouded behind her curtain of black hair
and empty eyes

hoping nothing will find her,
but everything always finds her

# River Song

Thought I buried it all
like the leaves in the fall
but it came back in a flood
and I'm drowning now.

I wasn't ready to see
what it would do to me,
how it would bleed me dry
but I'm drowning now.

I'm no boat on this river,
I made with my own tears.
And I can't change the past
or all of those lost years.
Don't ask me to sail it again.
I can't navigate this fall with you.

It's time to let it go.
Just let it go.

So, I'm asking you now.
Let me sail through it somehow
and put it all away
because I'm drowning now.

Every day is a tight rope
from the past to my next hope.
There's no bridge to cross,
just a thin line on a journey to death.

So, I'm asking you now.
Let me sail through it somehow
and put it all away
because I'm drowning now.
It's time to let it go.
Please help me let it go.

I need to breathe.
Breathe into me.
Surface and survive.
Make this river my peace
and let it go.

So, I'm asking you now.
Let me sail through it somehow
and put it all away
because I'm drowning now.

# Mantra

I cannot stop at one
and that is why I must have none.

## Over

I knew it was over when you were no longer the subject of my stories, and reserving the ink in my pen meant more to me than giving you life on paper.

# Alone

I knew it was over when being alone felt more at home than being in your arms.

## Scream

I screamed into the wind.

She cried back,
drowning me in silence
with her sorrow.

# Vacation

here they come again
waiting in the shadows
ready to pull me into the abyss
pricking my fingertips in warning
as though I could run with the chains
anchoring my ankles

they wake me from sleep
distract me from purpose
enable me with their lies

no longer under my bed
no longer just in my head
but moving under my skin

static on every nerve
acid in every organ
dripping off my lips
back into my ears in a vicious cycle

wash, spin, repeat
wash, spin, repeat

how many times do I have to drown before I
let them go?

I could be so much more if I said goodbye

to the demons
to the past
to the vice-numbing poisons whose voices
are louder than mine

they are tired too

even monsters need a vacation
as they surf on salty tears

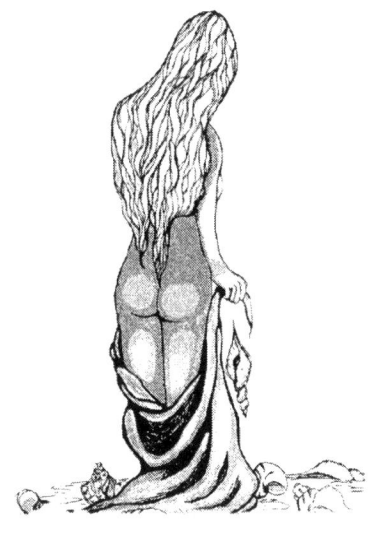

# Choices

If I'd chosen you,

I wouldn't be writing this today.

If I'd chosen you,

I would have given myself over to your making.

If I'd chosen you,

I would have accepted nothing more.

If I'd chosen you,

it would have been my fault

for allowing it to happen.

## Trust

Every betrayal of trust has been at the hands of those I believed were here to offer me mine.

# Thorns

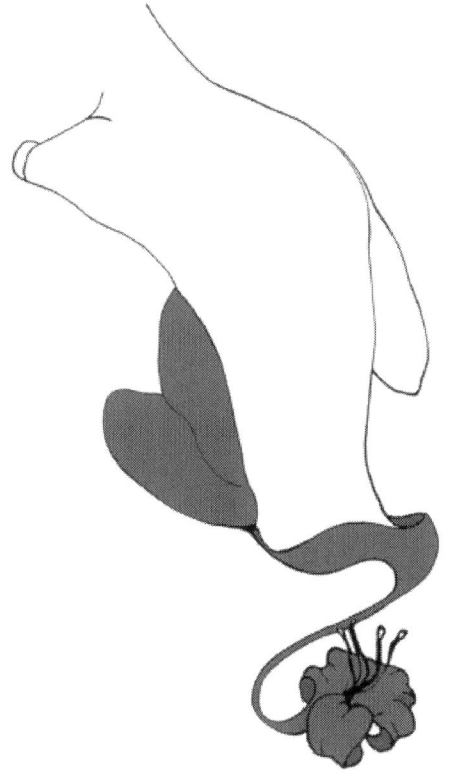

# Diagnosis

If this is my journey,

may I
travel
it with
grace.

## Reign

I would gift you my hope to wear like armor.

I would gift you my grace to satiate your soul.

I would gift you my strength to fight the battles that rage within your heart.

Whatever may come, I will wear your burdens like a crown and reign in your hell if it gives you a moment's peace.

# The Fool's Journey

the precipice before the leap
is not for the faint of heart

only a fool would dance off the edge, she said

but what a dance
what magic
what possibilities await you on your journey

for within the fall is the lesson
and from it, magic becomes the magician

forged with the arcana,
a sacred gift from the High Priestess herself

look within
look within,
she whispers in my ear

never fear
never fear
I am always near
never fear

Shufelt-Break & Bloom

I shall make you an Empress and from red-ripened hackberries,
fire will grow, swelling your belly
until you birth a new creation

no matter the pleasure,
all birth comes with pain, she reminds

flesh will tear from your sovereign womb
to release life abloom,
an Emperor,
a butterfly stretching its wings,
soaring to new heights,
kissing the sun

but what have you learned?
are you paying attention to the hierophants
with their mystery lessons?

some are lovers
some are friends
some will hurt you in the end

they are all mirrors,
a reflection of your past,
a portal to your present,
a woven tapestry from an infinite cosmic rug

as you twist
and turn
and scream
and cry
and burn

as flesh sears to one and then departs to
another in this life of meetings and partings

awaken in love and heartbreak

you are no longer the Fool
leaping haphazardly into the abyss
dancing free without trepidation

no
there are cracks in your vessel
there are wounds on your hands,
and deeper still are the scars that remain

take the reins of your chariot
gather all your strength
for that was just a taste, she whispers

your life is not random
it is not happenstance
becoming by chance outside of you

no
it is life manifesting out of your becoming

something you cannot possibly comprehend
nor accept until you sit within the seat of
your Soul and listen as the hermit would

life is a wheel,
cycles upon cycles,
patterns upon patterns,
a cosmic scale from which there are
choices, and what you choose, you become

be mindful, for every choice carries the
justice of karma

and in every karmic result is the possibility
of transformation not always seen as a gift
like a chrysalis hanging in surrender's repose

it is a death to let go,
to be in the ebb of temperance's flow


for, 'tis better to float against the current
than to fight the inevitable

she releases you

now is the moment of truth,
the ascension into authenticity
or descent into powerlessness,
to become stormbound to your demons
or reign as captain of your own ship

the tower you have built crumbles
as do your self-made delusions
as do all your ubiquitous allegories
until they lay crushed and chaste to seed anew

breathe
just breathe

open your eyes, she says
there is beauty amid chaos,
calm after the storm,
breakthroughs after breakdowns,
stars that shine after the darkest night,
hidden messages that surface in the moon's reflective glow

listen to the water ripple with its temporal voice

replace your fear with clarity kissed by the sun

it shines a light on your past and future self

this is the final act of judgment,
illuminating how you came to be,
where you are yet to go,
and as you rise, I place new words upon your tongue

look within
look within,
she whispers in your ear
tell me now the lessons you've longed to hear

the words once forgotten and misunderstood are now a mantra,
resolute within your mind

they pour off your tongue,
a gift from the Divine

never fear
never fear
I am a world of my making
never fear

# Breadcrumbs

I wasn't born this way, and until a few years ago, I thought I knew myself.

But life doesn't give you a rule book, and the future isn't written in stone.

The road we travel is a never-ending conundrum of choices.

And what we unlock is with the keys we forge from experience.

There are no failures in the game of life.

And the lies will run you ragged sometimes.

You'll tell them to yourself and make them stick like glue while the truth sits back in quiet reserve, waiting for you.

Rise
Fall
Forward
Retreat
The key ring is getting heavier.

So, don't let those keys weigh you down like an anchor.

Leave them on the path you travel just in case you get lost along your way.

## Speak to Me

Every moment I am going inward with reverence, like some hermit in the Tarot, exploring my ancestors' ancient memories and lost teachings.

They are traveling beneath this aging mortal veil, grieving regrets, with wounds so deep, I fear I may drown in their heartbreak.

## Sabotage

I am a work in progress, a never-ending conundrum of unfinished thoughts and unborn creations.

Laced together with undiscovered truths and self-imposed lies.

Forged in molten rage that never cools but longs for solidity.

A roadmap of unhealed scars leading to nowhere.

A portrait of unresolved pain trapped in a frame forged in inadequacy.

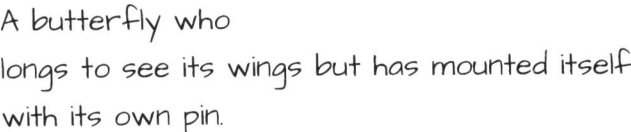

A butterfly who
longs to see its wings but has mounted itself with its own pin.

## Balance

I am a contradiction,
loath to be seen
while screaming naked
from the rooftops of my soul.

I wish to hide with the demons
who keep me bound as their lover
while transmuting their venomous gifts
of fear and rage into words
ripe with sovereignty.

The battle within me makes me weak,
but I feel strength in my surrender.

## Perfect

She was always drawn to broken things.

The teddy bear with one eye.

The doll with the cracked face.

Lonely, discarded objects that the world had dismissed.

It made her cry, knowing they were unloved.

To her, their brokenness made them beautiful.

It was no wonder that broken people would find her as she grew older.

For she was broken too, and it made it easy for her to love them as though they were children born from her own womb.

# Turn

I procrastinated from hope
to avoid disappointment.

# Escape

The woods are calling me.
I long to run until I am hidden among the crowning trees and buried under the fallen leaves.

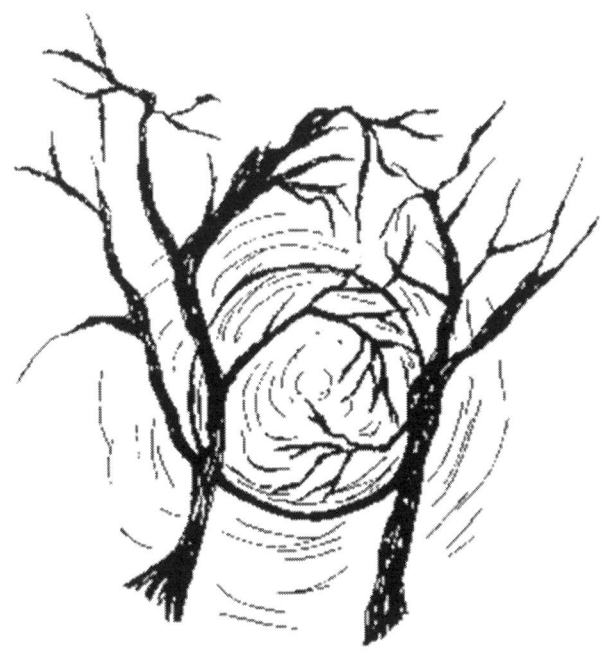

# No More

I'm sorry.

It shouldn't be this way.

It was selfish to bring you into a violent world hell-bent on its destruction-

a world full of warmongers who believe in profit over people and industry over the earth-

a world of false idols, spin doctors, and puppet masters.

Because once you burst into this big blue world, they see you as a commodity to buy and sell.

And when you serve your purpose, whether by awakening to the truth, or old age, they will dismiss you.

They will cheapen your existence to maintain their control.

They will judge your book by its cover.

They will manipulate you with their narratives, plant seeds of fear under your skin, turn love into poison, and faith into fear.

They may even wish you'd never been born.

Oh, the irony of the womb lovers.

I didn't understand this until I was much older.

Again, I'm sorry.

Why bring you into such a fucked-up place?

Some say it's because we dare to love- that love is the most potent antidote.

But as I become older, more awakened, or perhaps more dismissed, I realize the answer is hope.

Each generation hopes the next will be better than the last.

I know that's a heavy burden.

To say I've been there and done that is an understatement.

If you are hope incarnate, as we were the hope of the generation before, may your eyes open sooner.

May you be the change we couldn't or chose not to be before we believed the lie that we didn't matter.

## Punch-drunk

I drank in my madness like wine and let it fill the shallow spaces until I was too numb to recognize hope was drowning.

## Cracked

I'm walking on eggshells all the time,

then I think, I am the egg.

Fragile-

a shell as thin as tissue paper,

inside, a gelatinous, anxious mess.

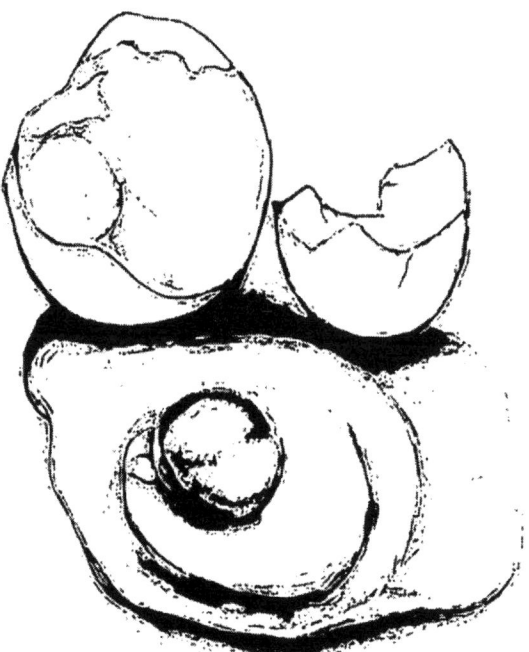

I know I could be good to somebody-

if not to others, at least to myself-

if I could keep from breaking.

I used to fry up one-liners, nutritious with wisdom.

I could scramble the shit out of a bad situation and turn it sunny side up in a jiffy.

I could create fresh dishes to feed my hungry soul and the souls of others.

I believed it too-

all the things I could create from one freshly hatched egg, let alone a dozen.

Now I feel separated-

mixed into old ingredients I didn't measure and should have discarded long ago.

Something I need to clean off the floor

## Once Upon a Time

Long ago, there was a fairytale about a young girl who fell in love with a boy whose hollow eyes were so deep in darkness that she drowned.

The author, who penned the story, used the memories of her heartbreak captured in an old inkwell and her skin as parchment.

The nib she fashioned from her bone, and from it flowed inky words dripping with sorrow.

When finished, she ripped the pages from her spine and burned them to ash, remembering not all stories end happily ever after.

# Cold Girl

I wish I could be the silent snow-

let it fill me with solitude

as it blankets the noise within me.

But I'm a cold girl with frost-bitten fingertips and winter's broken heart.

I can only imagine you from a distance

-an untouchable ache

born of the same material, yet worlds apart.

## Screaming Silent

You got tired of screaming,
and that's why you died.

I learned how to scream,
so I could live.

## Pedestal

Nothing is sadder than what you perceived as perfect coming to an end.

It will take you back to your first loss and that gut-wrenching moment when you felt yourself spiraling into unbreachable grief.

## Anxiety's Pull

caught in the eventide of my thoughts

drowning in the resonating undertow of my chaos

I drink in the shadows of my bitter wine

I feast on nettled fruit pies, using ingredients purchased and grown from shared recipes and others of my making

until my belly aches and bloats

until thorns breach from under my nails

until a thousand saturnine seeds spew from my bruised, teeth-bitten lips,

releasing me from this copious hell-

then and only then did I empty this vessel,

and in the silence, hear my voice leading me to salvation

# War

It's hard to create
when my soul is tired.

Even now, I fight to find my words.
My heart is an empty drum,

yet every corner of this shell is cracking open, pushed to the brink with fears I can no longer repress.

I cannot hold my enemies back when a silent war rages in every tissue, echoing destruction yet to be seen.

While much of life is ephemeral,
what goes unresolved is eternal.

# Grief

Spiral down into the deepest part of me
where the ocean ceases to end,
where light fails to penetrate,
and cold envelopes everything
like a weighted blanket.

That is where you will find me,
a sunken vessel with a broken compass,
drowning in the brine of my tears.

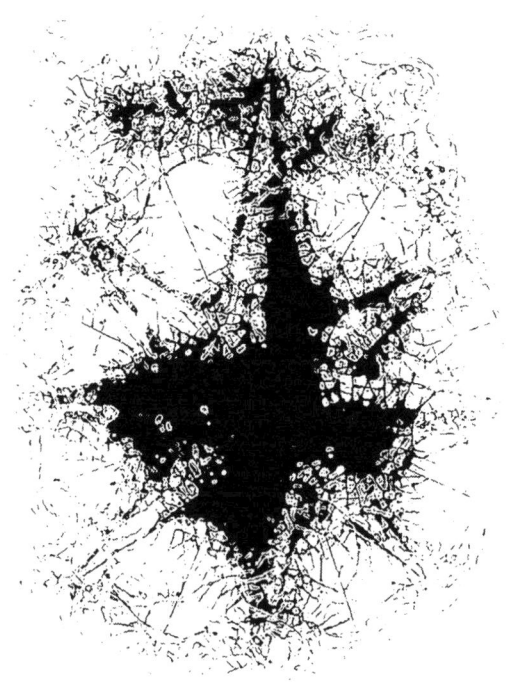

## Safe Place

Open your scars to your raw, visceral pain.

Hold nothing back.

Let your memories bleed over your tongue and into my mouth.

Release the imprints through the sting of salty tears until they leave nothing to clot.

And when you are done, let my arms be your dressing.

Fold into me until your ghosts disappear like the fragments of a retreating dream.

Allow me to be the resting place where all your pain comes to die.

# Empty

It happened gradually, the way fine lines betide a face without notice.

I gave away pieces-
some small, others large, to strangers, friends, and lovers, hoping to be seen and heard.

I bargained and bartered, fearing loss and death.

I sold when ego and vanity ensured something better.

I allowed theft when I failed to see value in what I had.

I lost because of carelessness and distraction.

Whatever I had left, I scattered, hoping the trail would lead me back to the most important piece worth saving.

Myself

## Missing

You entered my mind today, and I saw you had disappeared.

Strange how I would feel your presence but be unaware of your exit.

And I wondered how I had missed this transition?

Then the guilt seeped under my skin like slow-growing ivy on a stone wall.

I couldn't shake the emptiness even though I could feel you everywhere.

# From P to M

If you peel back the sky,
you will find me
with my pallet of ocean hues,
walking canvases of sandy beaches,
while taking in majestic views.

My camera is always with me.
Funnel cakes and corn dogs scent the air.
I bring images to life in an instant
and Counting Crows music plays
everywhere.

No memory is lost or faded.
No image is static or grey.
Only scrapbooks of places I have been
and those where I longed to stay.

Pictures of us and those I love.
Dancing with you in the rain.
Hearing you when you talk to me.
Painting away your tears and pain.

If you are lost, peel back the sky,

that is where I will always be.
Watching over you like I did on Earth
until you come home to me.

# Rabbit Soup

You won't find me chasing rabbits or at the bottom of a rabbit hole.

Instead, I'll be a pot of soup, made by hands fresh from the kill-

with too many chefs to name, but who have all come to stir the pot.

It's a pot I forged from clenched fists, unsaid words, and madness not always of my making.

Sometimes it leaks.

Other times, it overflows.

There are even times when I have found it empty.

I'd like to say the contents taste good, but I'd be lying to you and myself.

There's too much acid, leaving it bitter.

Too many storms, leaving it salty.

And far too many things I care not to name, leaving it toxic.

I sometimes think I should start over with a stronger vessel-

one which contains better ingredients
crafted with kinder hands-


one where the rabbits aren't screaming.

Hers

We are all Death's children,
riding out this journey in bodies hell-bent on our destruction.

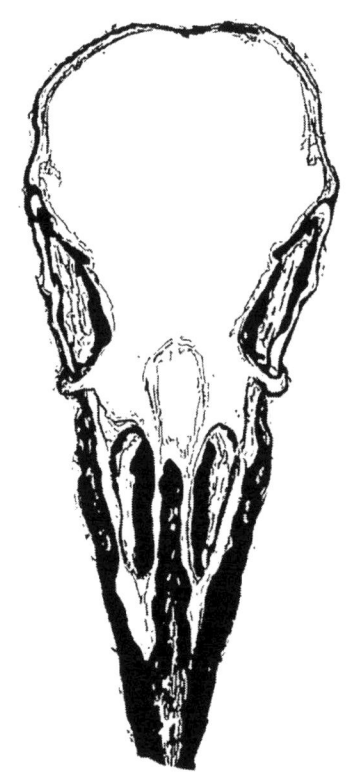

## Predictive Text Poetry

I will not be there in the morning
or the next.

If you need me,
I'll be in your room of shadows, dancing with
the memories of us.

## Haunted

listen to the empty house
imprints seeping through cracked plaster
ghostly voices lamenting torment from leaky pipes

all the unsaid things
now revealed through peeling wallpaper
unhindered by age
while everything neglected remains buried under layers of ugly paint

wood-worn floorboards sag with the weight of what once was,
what could have been,
what still remains

backscatter memories linger like cigarette smoke,
ancient reminders of bad choices,
insincere promises
and pain so present,
it cries remembrance in every rusty door hinge

maybe it wants to be heard
the way we want to be heard,

in our creaking, worn-out bones,
in our thoughts unhindered by age,
in buried regrets now quivering off our
rusty lips,
in what we can no longer contain behind our
leaky eyes

what once was,
what could have been,
what still remains

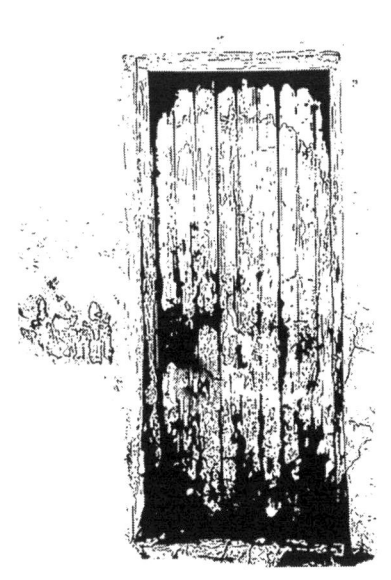

# Soul Searching

Elusive—

I searched for you in books, flesh, cinema, Guru, and Guide.

Veiled—

You journeyed under my skin on an inky highway.

You spoke to me in random songs and ignited me through match-struck epiphanies and lucid dreams.

And when I would not listen, you pricked warnings on the back of my neck.

You seeded fear with knife jabs in my already leaky gut.

When I blamed you, you broke me open like over-ripened fruit cloyed in heartbreak and awakened me in the guise of disease.

I'm here! I've always been here!

When I saw you reflected,

I saw myself.

A gift, not of anger, not of fear, but of love.

I keep the scars as treasured reminders.

Should I become lost, they will be a roadmap back to us.

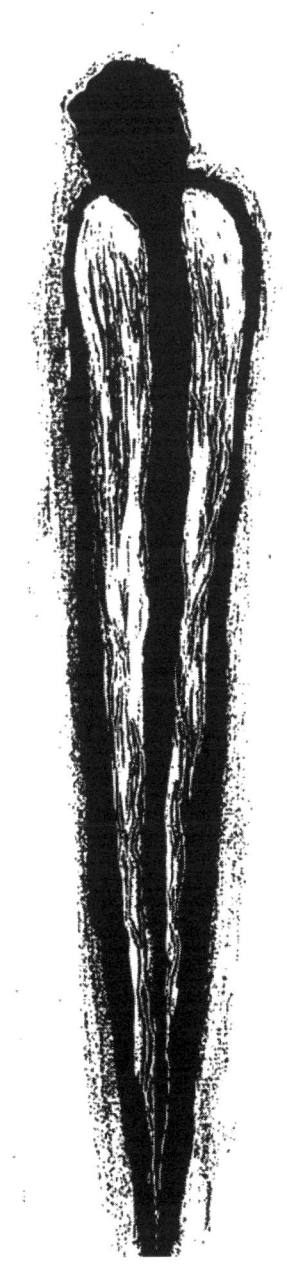

Shouldering the weight of unspoken pain
under the veil of weak smiles, I
realize I am truth behind self-imposed lies,
violently laced together from imprints
I've yet to burn. Still, I find my
voice, hidden deep in layers of doubt. I'm
on a quest to silence the demons
raging war on the battlefield of my mind.

## Moonstruck

the moonstruck girl who gave her throat over to wolves

the one who worshiped at godless feet and found salvation in their pretty lies

the one who came willingly to sacrificial tables in anticipation of melancholy breakfasts and sinful desserts

the one who allowed the sacred sea to baptize her, only to drown in its profane depths

too many people got her desperation rather than what they deserved

she will never be that girl again

Precious Things

Between yesterday's shadows and the light of tomorrow, I found armor disguised as hope, waiting to awaken my warrior soul.

## Avoidance

It was easier to give myself away than to live with a stranger I didn't want to know.

# Blooms

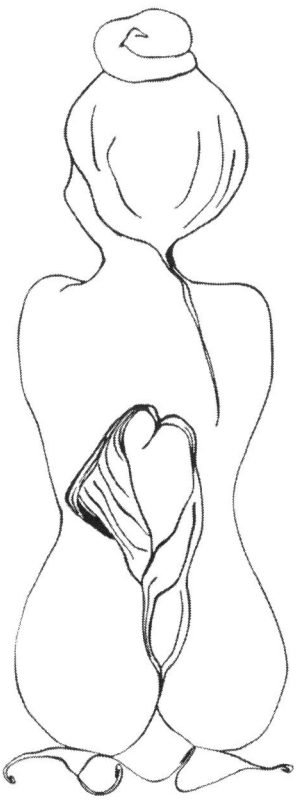

And I would search a million lifetimes
Never doubting our love.
Desirous of time for which there is no end
Reverent in a soul connection
Even the heavens envy in their curious gaze
Whilst silently blessing with humbling grace

## Stories

You needn't say a word. You spoke volumes upon my skin as though it were parchment and your fingers were the pen.

# Gemels

Some stories exist long before the paper on which they are written.

I believe we were always weaving our way toward each other.

We searched through labyrinths of dark matter, battlefields of broken bones, and splintered promises, until the rising and falling of our individual storms crashed together like the inosculation of tree roots forming one soul.

That is the story of you and me becoming us.

Shufelt-Break & Bloom

## The Allegory of Secret Places

What mysteries await beneath the penumbra of ivory lace?

Ah, the contour of cinnamon lips that limn an arcane wonderland with the salt of a melancholy kiss.

# Elements

I sank into your skin, covered by shadows of unknown possibilities, twisting and turning within your limbs until we crowned out the world above.

I was easy to break like a paper nautilus not carried by the waves
but thrashed by storms crashing against the seashore.

And you broke me wide open, the way spirited horses are known to break, releasing salty tears filled with fear and lost imprints laden with cruelty.

In those melancholy moments, you explored all my liminal places as though they were a hiraeth you longed for, but wished to forget.

Shufelt-Break & Bloom

You held me up and observed every broken piece of my soul like a child with a curious treasure-

searching for my hidden wings, but fearful, if found, I would fly away.

I never knew you were looking for your own wings through me.

## The Promises of Evermore

tell me a story
about midnight
and stardust,
about daydreams
and bloodlust

feed me grapes
fermented in sin
as our fingers dance
on unrepentant skin

as dusky shadows
hang low like memory eaves,
let's reminisce the time away
on a bed of velvet leaves

for once upon a time,
not so long ago,
our thorns were lovely roses
blooming a youthful glow

time has endeavored to alter,
through the salt of winter's kiss,
the gifts that we remember
and others choose to dismiss

so let us bathe in twilight
and read love's written lore,
still ripe beneath our inky veins,
the promises of evermore

# You

In the unspoken words behind your eyes, I saw you.

In the smiles that danced between us, I heard you.

In the lingering brush of unseen fingertips, I wanted you.

And in the quiet stillness of time that linked us, I became you.

## Stargaze

The night envelopes me in starlight kisses,
promising more than any dawn can deliver.

# Wanderlust

Dance me in the twilight hours when the moon awaits her dawning, and the sun escapes her calling.

Unwind me inch by inch and stroke by stroke until I leave all my broken offerings with the hands of time.

From my barred throat, devour my severed soul until it is unknown and forgotten.

I want to become serene in my wanderlust with you.

Perhaps I've been blessed with an
Angel in disguise. What other
Truth could there be in your eyes?
Rumor has it that you are a teacher
In heart and in mind, charged with love-
Centered
Kindness to all humankind.

# Eternal

There has never been a moment when I did not love you.
From inception to conception, until the dirge of death and beyond the etheric realms.
I will always love you.

## October Gives Birth

With numb fingers and frozen toes,
October dances a dirge of death
to songs created by her crows
while winter watches with bated breath.

Variegated leaves crush beneath her feet-
chased by dusky twilight shadows.
The Queen of Faerie, she will greet
with her book of lost tomorrows.

She feeds on acorns, arsenic, and old lace,
washing it down with herbal tea
while candlelight veils her aging face,
lined with memories of what will never be.

As her reign now ushers a somber close,
she births a child with delight,
whose frost blue lips recite winter prose
of mother's wisdom to mortal's enlight.

# Rain

When the rain falls,
drink me in
until I drown the chaos
of soiled thoughts damning your flow.

When the
storms
come,
drink me in
until your
empty
vessel,
satiated
with love,
overflows,
and your
strangled
roots
breach the
surface,
to swim in
freedom.

# Healing

However much time the hurt took space in your heart, give as much, if not more, to healing.

Healing is a sacred journey.

Travel the time needed with reverence.

# Poisoned

I brought a pen and journal to every treatment but found it impossible to write.

No words came.

I couldn't think.

I couldn't feel.

I was numb.

I could only sit and watch the cherry Kool-Aid liquid move turtle slow through the IV connected to the port in my chest.

I refused to call it anything but a miracle even though I knew it was poison.

Those in the know called it the Red Devil.

And after it moved through me, killing everything in its path, it turned the water red before I flushed it away.

It would take my hair,

my extra weight,

my monthly blood,

at times my sanity,

but it would also take my cancer.

Eventually, I would pick up my pen again and I would write.

And as I wrote, I felt the poison withdraw from my veins into the pen's shaft as though I had sliced them open with the nib.

Then I discovered the power that resides in the poisoned pen.

May I always remember some poisons heal as well as kill.

## Razor

I watched my hair drift
to the floor like dried leaves
falling from an autumn tree.

The loss hastened
by metal separating
threads sewn to lies.

Lies about beauty.
Lies about femininity.
Lies about youth.

Naked truth stared at me,
dropping any remaining pretense
to the floor.

A vanity shield, gone forever.
Gone
like my monthly blood.

I am Winter,
and death walks beside me,
giving me strength and power in this journey.

## Surrender

When I relinquished the need to know, I found the word surrender vibrating on my lips. And when I understood its power, it freed me from a thousand sleepless nights and unknown fears.

## Girl in a Box

Look at the girl in her little box, surrounded by paper walls decorated with crayon marks.

Head above the rim like she's treading water. Sailing to adventure land with her picture books and tiny plastic people.

Mama took that picture long ago.
Funny how children love to play in boxes the way cats do.

As children, our boxes are gateways to Narnia, rocket ships to the moon, secret forts of make-believe, and ships navigating stormy seas.

At 52, my cardboard box has plaster walls, and a new shingled roof courtesy of my insurance company.

I still sail stormy seas in my fortresses of solitude.

It's become a quiet escape from outside world atrocities.

Gone are the crayons, replaced by expensive artist paints.
Gone are the picture books, replaced by poetry books and classic novels.
Gone are the plastic people, replaced by flesh and blood beings, fur babies, and memories.

I no longer wish to put my head above its eaves, but sometimes, I peek out the window to watch the foxes play in the garden.

I'm still just a girl in a box.

Still imagining fantastical places from inside a larger box with more walls on which to paint my journeys.

## Umbra

It is in her; I long to find myself.
It is from her; I long to run away.
My coldest winter bites at me until I recognize her healing light.
In my awakening self,
I float in the arms of her release.

## Goals

I seek not the approval of the masses but forever strive toward the contentment of my soul.

# Swallow

the birch eyes are watching
what the swallow caught today
no charm could stall or stop him
as he merrily flew away

no rook or raven mocked him
the higher and higher he flew
his prize between a dragonfly's wings,
still fresh with morning dew

his burst of fluid wingbeats
his acrobatic flight
the glossy blue of plumage
an omen to Sailor's sight

then he circled back toward me
and dove at the ground
my breath caught a moment
when he dropped what he had found

not a tear did it suffer,
his released gift to me
the dragonfly landed in my hand,
alive as it could be

Shufelt-Break & Bloom

away the swallow flew,
taking to the sky once more
in its flight of Divinity
and returned to me nevermore

# Here

In every breath of wind
that caresses your cheek,
in every song from the blackbird
that sings remembrance in your ears,
in every carefully timed leaf
that dances before your eyes,
I am with you.

# No

Sometimes, "no" is a silent scream

Sometimes, "no" is an echo coming back to your lips from the past.

Sometimes, "no" appears after the well of tears have finally dried up.

Sometimes, "no" is what you hear when you finally realize you are enough.

Forgiveness

When the freedom of peace is worth more than seeking the spoils of war.

## Weave World

I am a woven world,
sewn from countless threads,
spooled from possibility,
with needles forged
in molten memories.

## With or Without You

enough time has passed between then and now for me to realize nothing truly disappears

and while the feeling of love, loss, pain, or grief may lessen, it will find resurrection in the most unexpected ways

in an all too familiar stranger's face,
in song lyrics never acknowledged but are now an undelivered letter from the past,
in a benign object made worthy again by a certain slant of light

Nothing ever dies
it just transforms

coming back around
to remind us
that neither they nor we
will ever be lost or forgotten

# Solitude

I'd rather retreat into the solitude of my soul than be with those who have shut the door on their own.

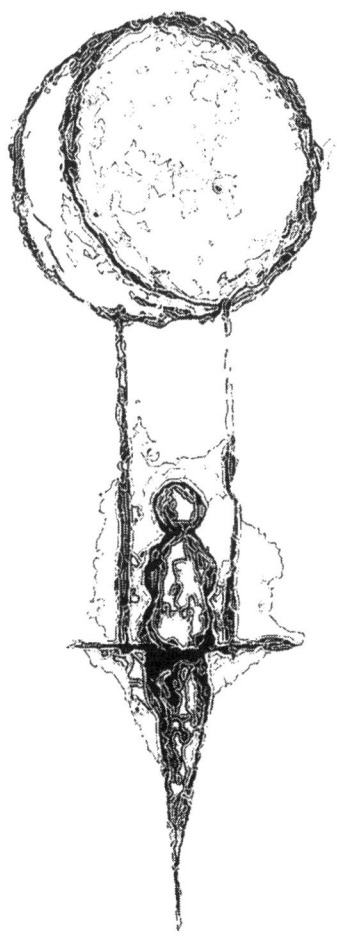

## I Wish for Silence

I wish for silence—
where I am undisturbed by noise pollution and fallacious chatter

an Amity where fiery vitriolic words extinguish to ash

a sacred place where demonic imprints are mute in reverence, healing lamented wounds without recompense

I wish for silence—
where love shone in the eyes needs no words yet conveys a canvas mellifluous with meaning

where the lightest touch sings a thousand sensations under the skin

where the quiescent chrysalis births euphonious mysteries from the infinite universe

I wish for silence so ubiquitous it becomes like the air I breathe, resonating in its own unconscious vibration heard only through the filter of my soul

# Rise

watch it burn
watch us strike a match to their hate
watch us throw gasoline on their
combustible supplications roiling with lies

better to burn it to ash
than letting
it burn us
alive

that is
where
truth
begins

and from
the ash, we
birth a
revolution

this is
where we
rise

## Looking in the Mirror

*I'm sorry*
I took you for granted.
I fed you lies for breakfast
and bathed you in doubt.

*I'm sorry*
for not listening
when all you needed was silence.

*I'm sorry*
for filling your head with fear
because it felt safer than faith.

*I'm sorry*
I couldn't see you were enough.

# Art of Pain

The pain you inflicted upon me became a masterpiece sculpted in strength.

# The Art of Healing

I'm an artist.
Whatever the subject,
there are plenty of hidden erasures,
mistakes covered by layers of muddy paint,
hours, perhaps years of attempted failures,
starts, and stops.

I can tell you without hesitation that all art
has an ugly phase before it's released.

That is why I'm telling you now,
allow the erasures,
allow the mistakes,
allow the mud,
allow the failed starts and lingering stops.
It's all part of the process.

Because healing is a lot like art.
Anything we wish to realize or release must
go through the ugly phase.

And some pieces will always
be works in progress.

# Break & Bloom

everything breaks
everything falls
leaving traces of itself behind

seeds rise from fallen trees
spores release from decay
letting go but not forgotten
transforming with trust

you can do this
you can rise
seed a new day
let it go
release it to trust

brush your teeth
comb your hair
I see you
behind that beautifully broken stare

even when you feel numb,
even when you think you can break no further,
those transient moments are seeds

new paths birthing

from what has fallen,
blooming from what has broken

through trust,
another day is worth seeding
because *you* are worth seeding

*you* are worth birthing
*you* are worth being
broken but blooming
beautiful and seen

still there
still rising
still trying
still feeling

still

# First Frost

Death paid me a winter's visit.
She never knocked as she had a key.
Her intentions were implicit,
though she spoke no initial words to me.

Shaped in darkness and from fear,
the key, she anchored in my breast.
Not a damning word from my lips appeared,
nor any miracles did I request.

Her time with me was more than a season,
and why, I never did question.
I knew she was there for a vital reason
as a soul teacher with a mystery lesson.

It was not Death who took my hair.
It was not Death who racked my bones with pain.
She simply waited to see if I would care
or turn on her with blame.

When I chose to send her love instead,
she looked at me and smiled.
Death is not something to fear or dread,

for she only comes to protect her child.

We are all her children; I heard her say
on a journey back to her tomb.
Releasing this life of sorrow and decay
in the peace of her loving womb.

I do not fear her, for she means no harm.
And when she comes to call again,
I will welcome her with open arms
as a known and trusted friend.

## Death is a Collector

I think Death is a collector, looking upon us as works of art to warm her walls and as books full of melancholy poetry to crack her heart for all eternity.

## Kintsukuroi

In a disposable world,
my vessel is broken and imperfect.

I have scars above and below my breasts,
under my arm,
and some scars are hidden
so deep even I can't find them.

But I am not broken.
I am filled with gold.

My core melts
the swords I've swallowed,
filling my veins,
fusing my scars,
turning tainted blood into molten honey,
feeding my soul with rich insight-

crafting a vessel
more valuable than any work of art.

Do not let the naysayers question yourself

Or the voices in your head fill you with fear

Underneath it all, it is your journey

Because you are unlike anyone else

Trust the magic within you and rise

## Battleground

Don't let her soft demeanor
and gentle smile fool you.
She's been a General in her share of wars
and won more battles than the lines
around her eyes.

## January

life can turn on a dime
shake you from your slumbering grave
strip you naked in its storm
suck the air from your lungs
shock you to silence
with blood in your mouth,
head dizzy in its wake

now you are present
wide open and vulnerable
with veins so lead sodden,
you fear the slightest movement
will shatter you like glass

and you will shatter,
left with wounds so
deep the memories
will surface as scars

but those scars will
tell you something
else

you survived

# Baggage

I've walked the liminal space between the past and the present, unpacking suitcases filled with insecurity and all the fearful things I never wanted to witness in the light of day.

It's a brave task to dive into these murky bogs of misbelief.

It's difficult to taste shadow's bitterness on your tongue and then swallow the imprints as nourishment.

It's a warrior who willingly sacrifices cleaved skin to the past's pricking thorns, only to bleed out the chaos into the clotting ashes of yesteryear so they may bury it in sanity's sarcophagus.

# Aching Wisdom

On the days I fear how close I came to death, the scars remind me I survived.

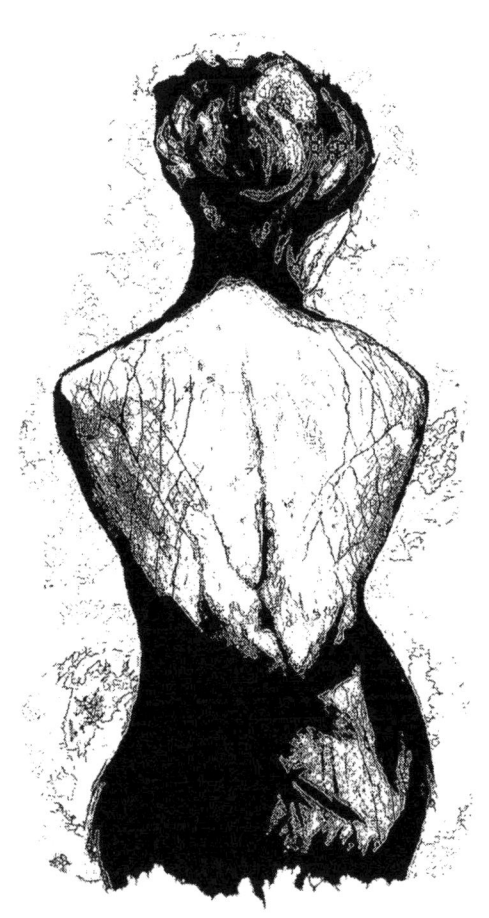

## Queen of Hell

Battle your madness with a poetic tongue.

Weave its whisperings like golden threads through your hair.

Wear your shadow like a second skin and forge your tears into a sacred crown.

But make no mistake, you rule the demons of your hell and not the other way around.

# Warrior

A month before the invader settled in her breast, she dreamt she was a blacksmith making swords for battle.

Everyone called her a warrior, though she'd never been to war and didn't have a violent bone in her body.

Yet there she was, going to war with herself.

And she saw her dream weapons turn into needles.

She saw the molten silver liquefy red as it pumped into her chest.

She imagined the toxins coursing through her veins were magic, and the rays that burned her breast were of the sun.

No tears did she shed when the vanity stripped free from her scalp.

She gave both over to her ancestors, accepting the losses that would eventually become her battle scars.

When acid formed sores in her mouth, she spoke no vengeful words and made no promises to her God.

Instead, she lay in the dark sarcophagus of her thoughts while Death stood watching nearby.

How close was she to her end date?

That innocuous date she passed each year, never realizing the place card it held for her somewhere in the cosmos.

Did it feel different from the other 364 days?

Was she too busy with life to notice?

Was it more peaceful or challenging?

Would she celebrate it like a birthday when it came time to leave this earthly plane?

Death laughed and squeezed her hand before it departed.

She wasn't a warrior like they all said.

She was a woman on a journey who would always wonder why Death whispered, "not today."

## To be a Book

I wonder if I could be a book?
Exchange my mottled skin for the amber-hued, sweet-scented pages, a commodity I would give freely to last longer.

We are similar; this book and I, with our cracking spine, tattered edges, and dog-eared tales.

We both had a once beautiful cover, now worn from age, made fragile by abuse, forgotten by neglect, but perhaps treasured in love.
What will we remember?
The once resilient layers now filled with fading inky memories and overused lines?
Or the memories of what was inside?

Still ripe with imaginaries.
Still fresh and childlike.
Forever young in thoughts and pictures, never aging, only transcending time.

Would the imaginaries allow me to melt into their world?

A world where mushrooms tower overhead like trees.
Where bees become chariots.
Where thistles become crowns and hawthorn needles, swords.
Where sun-bleached animal bones become armor, and autumn leaves are a roadmap of possibilities.

When I die, bury me with a book like this so I may live forever within its story.

# Wonderland Never Dies

Despite what the trappings of time have endeavored to alter, I still find magic in secret gardens and lost fairytales. I still embrace madness and wear it like a crown while stepping fool-heartedly into my Wonderland.

Shufelt-Break & Bloom

Special thanks to–

Mira Hadlow–As Muses Burn. Thank you for the beautiful foreword and your continued support and encouragement. It means more than I can ever convey.

To my college professor, Jeffrey Greene, whenever I doubt myself, I open your book To the Left of the Worshiper and read the inscription you wrote to me. Thank you for seeing my potential as a poet long before I saw it in myself.

## About the Artist

Trisha Leigh Shufelt is a self-taught artist and author, wife, mother, and cancer survivor.

Author/Artist Works Include
The Poe Tarot
The Everglow
Schiffer Publishing/RedFeatherMBS

Indie Published works include-
Liminal Lines- Poetry & Prose
Liminal Lessons- Poetry & Art

Indie Published under the pen
Andaleigh Archer include-
The Underwood Wicked Fairytale Series
The Promise ~A Faerie's Tale
Red Cinder Swan
Wicked Thorns
Little Red

You can find out more about Trisha at
www.artinsoul.org

Made in the USA
Middletown, DE
10 September 2022

72627627R00117